GOD Can Be Your Coach

GOD

Can Be Your Coach

Creating a Powerful, Personal and Practical Relationship with the Divine

By Wade Galt

Possibility Infinity Publishing

ISBN 978-1-934108-34-5

To GOD…

My Coach and Divine Inspiration.

To Mom…

My First Human Spiritual Coach.

To Debbie Ford and everyone in the Integrative Coaching Program…

My Human Inspiration.

Ask and you shall receive.

Create More Joy, Happiness, Love, Peace and Purpose in Your Life.

So many of us have been taught to pray or meditate... Yet so many of us can't seem to use these simple techniques to create the relationship with the Divine that we most desire.

This lack of connection to the divine can lead us to feel powerless, lost, confused and even abandoned by the divine and the world.

One simple assumption (and perhaps error) can prevent our attempts from connecting...

Many of us believe (perhaps incorrectly) that the although the Divine might listen to us, that it is not possible for us to receive clear guidance and direction from the Divine.

If we believe that we can only speak to the Divine, but never hear, it might be very difficult (even impossible) for us to truly relate with the Divine. After all, if we can't communicate back and forth with a person (or being), how can we really relate with them? If we have to try and guess what they are communicating to us, at best we will have a mysterious or confusing relationship filled with many misunderstandings.

Communicating to the Divine and receiving guidance does not need to be so complicated.

If we can learn to get quiet enough to silence the thoughts in our mind (at least temporarily), it becomes possible for us to listen to (and yes, hear) the quiet but powerful Divine voice inside us and receive the guidance, support and direction we seek.

Connecting with the Divine can be very simple.

Try this right now if you like...

- ➤ Open your mind and your heart to the possibility that you can connect with the divine.
- ➤ Decide that you would like to connect with the divine, and invite the divine to guide you in this process.
- ➤ Close your eyes and silently breathe in and out, focusing on your breath.
- ➤ Count to 3 as you breathe in, and count to 3 as you breathe out.
- ➤ Do this for 30 seconds (5 times in and 5 times out).
- ➤ Ask the divine to guide you with your inner voice and let you know if you can connect with the divine.
- ➤ Breathe in and out for 30 more seconds.
- ➤ Notice how you feel.
- ➤ Open your eyes.

What would your life be like if you could connect with the divine to receive guidance, love and support whenever and wherever you choose?

How much more Joy, Happiness, Love, Peace and Purpose could you create in your life?

This book in an invitation for you to start connecting and creating the life you most desire... Starting Today!

These Ideas Work For Me...

I wouldn't call them beliefs because I'm not attached to them. I'm not ready to kill or die to prove I'm right or that someone else is wrong. This is not dogma, so there's no need for anyone to argue. I'm not suggesting I'm right or others are wrong. I may be incorrect. I'm not saying I hold the only truth, the ultimate truth, or even truth.

This book is a collection of ideas that feel true to me, that inspire me, and that work for me (based on what I can see in my life). I'd love to hear how these and other ideas work for you. I see this as a two-way learning relationship that we can both learn from. I'm not the teacher. You're not the student. We're just two people exploring ideas about the divine in hope of improving our lives and the world.

Please Accept My Humility and My Grandiosity

It is my only intention that this work brings you closer to peace, love, joy, happiness, and a greater connection with the divine. Please excuse my limitations as a writer as I attempt to do this. It is not my intention to make anyone feel wrong, uncomfortable, that they need to change, or feel anything other than fully loved, accepted and supported.

Please accept my grandiosity in wanting to address such a huge and important subject (and any apparent presumption that I'm right). Please also accept my humility in doing my best to make myself vulnerable by sharing something I think will make the world a better place. I honor all those people, organizations, religions, beliefs, rituals, and everything else that seeks to do the same,

At the same time, I remain excited, open-hearted and open-minded to seeing how we may grow, evolve, and change how we relate with the divine and each other to bring about even more peace, love, and happiness.

Table of Contents

Notice

This book is about connecting with the divine and receiving divine wisdom. The author believes the knowledge and wisdom in this book are useful for anyone who seeks to enhance his or her connection with the divine. As with any discipline, results improve over time with consistent and focused practice.

The ideas and techniques presented in this book are not in any way intended to be a substitute for the advice of a physician or other licensed health care practitioner. If you are involved in psychotherapy, counseling or any other therapeutic relationship, it is advised that you not terminate treatment without consulting your therapist.

Any answer(s) or perceived guidance derived from the use of these methods should not be followed if it (1) harms any person or persons or (2) violates any local, state, federal or international law. Neither the author nor the publishers shall be liable or responsible to any person or entity for any loss or damage caused, or alleged to have been caused, directly or indirectly by the information or ideas contained, suggested, or referenced in this book.

It is the author's intention that this work leads the reader to a more powerful, personal, and practical relationship with the divine. The author believes the divine is the source of the answers he receives, and suggests that readers arrive at their own conclusions after using the techniques.

GOD Can Be Your Coach

First Contact

When I was 4 years old, I felt completely comfortable with the idea that I could communicate with God. ("God" was the name I learned to use when speaking of the divine). I knew God was there for me, and I knew I would always be okay because I had this really cool friend named "God" who was looking out for me. Somewhere between the ages of 4 and 30, I decided to become "smart." I learned a lot of "brilliant" things, and received a great deal of attention for being intellectually "gifted". It seems that while I was busy being "smart" I forgot some extremely important things along the way.

After I shared this book with my mother for her to read, she related a story to me that made me realize that it has taken me 26 years to remember something I knew when I was 4.

One day when we were at church, I told her that God had told me something.

"What did he tell you?" she asked.

"He told me that he loves me," I replied knowingly. I knew I was important enough for the divine to care about. I did not have to worry about whether or not "He" was actually a "he" or not, and I didn't have to put myself down by telling myself I wasn't good enough for God to care about or communicate with.

Without any thinking, intellectualizing, rationalizing, or justifying, I knew one simple truth – God loves me and wants to be my friend. I didn't know many of the "brilliant" things I know today, and I didn't have the educational degrees and letters after my name that "prove" I'm smart, but I did know something more important, more powerful, more simple, more wise, and more life-changing than anything I've learned since. ***The divine loves me, and I can have a personal relationship with the divine.***

Put another way, ***"I'm good enough to be friends with God."***

We're all good enough to be friends with God.

GOD Is My Coach

I mean that literally, not figuratively. When I need guidance, I go to God. When I need clarity, I go to God. When I need peace, I go to God. When I need encouragement, I go to God.

If you prefer a different name for the source of all creation, then please substitute it for the word "God." A rose by any other name is still a rose. The essence and the nature of the divine are not changed by the names we choose. It doesn't matter what name we use for God. We have been taught different names, but the divine is the divine.

By profession, I am a personal and team coach. I help people and organizations create what they most desire in life, and I facilitate their attainment of their dreams, goals and desires. People experience remarkable breakthroughs in their lives as a result of working with me. There are many other people who are also personal coaches – some do it for a living and some just do it naturally. A coach is anyone who helps you be a better you. A coach can be a teacher, a parent, a supervisor, a friend, a spiritual leader, or anyone who helps another person grow.

A coach can also be a divine being – if we choose. *We can decide to allow the divine to guide and direct our lives. We can use the most powerful force in the universe to amplify the love, success, enjoyment and fulfillment we experience. We can be more effective, powerful and compassionate people by receiving guidance from the source of creation.*

And we can do all of this without making anybody else wrong. We can live in harmony with those who have different spiritual or religious beliefs. We do not need to make any such organization or institution wrong. All we need to do is invite the divine to be a greater part of our lives. Placing our energy anywhere else (such as trying to make someone else wrong) limits the amount of energy we can devote to connecting with the divine.

We can also choose how much influence we want the divine to have over our lives. In fact, we do this already. We decide how much we allow ourselves to be influenced by the divine. We also choose how much we're going to be affected by the organizations, religions and people who look to support the work of the divine. Please notice I have separated the two. The followers of the divine are not the same as the divine. I'm seeking to receive guidance directly from the divine... not from a spiritual leader, organization or religion. I seek to go straight to the source of truth in order to minimize human error.

I suggest you read this book in the same light. If what you know, through your DIRECT EXPERIENCE of YOUR relationship with the divine, does or does not agree with the contents of this book, trust YOUR DIRECT EXPERIENCE. ***The purpose of this book is to lead you to a better relationship with the divine***. It is neither my intention to limit your experience of the divine nor suggest there is only one way to the divine. It is a bit like trying to explain with words what sugar tastes like or how a rose smells. ***Words help, but only direct experience leads to knowing.***

I invite you to do three things as you read this book.

1) ***Temporarily forget everything you know about the divine and assume you know nothing.*** (When our cup is full of what we "know", we have no room for new wisdom).

2) ***In whatever way you find comfortable, ask or invite the divine to help you reach greater clarity and understanding about how you can be most true to the divine part of you.*** (Through this book or any other way you find comfortable and effective).

3) ***Rely on YOUR DIRECT EXPERIENCE of the divine to guide you in determining the truth.*** For the remainder of this book, temporarily let go of or ignore the opinions of all other people and institutions. This way your relationship with the divine will be based on <u>your direct experience</u>, not someone else's belief.

Experiential Exercises

This book contains a brief and powerful experiential exercise at the end of each chapter. These exercises are intended to help you to directly experience the words in this book. They, like this book, are simply one way of experiencing this material. They, like this book, are optional but recommended.

I encourage you to do these exercises as they are written the first time you read the book, and then customize them to best suit your needs. When you make them your own, they will become even more powerful for you.

At the end of the book, there is contact information for the author so you may share what you have done with the process and what you have experienced, if you like.

Enjoy... if you choose.

Experiential Exercise #1

> ➤ **Set an intention to connect with the divine, and invite the divine to guide you in this process. ***

> ➤ **Open up to the possibility that you can connect with the divine.**

> ➤ Close your eyes and silently breathe in and out, focusing on your breath.

> ➤ Count to 3 as you breathe in, and count to 3 as you breathe out.

> ➤ Do this for 60 seconds (10 times in and 10 times out).

> ➤ **Notice how you feel.**

> ➤ Open your eyes.

* An intention is simply a desire you wish to have fulfilled. Setting an intention to connect with the divine simply means declaring a desire to have the divine connect with you for this exercise. This declaration can be made silently within you.

Who Am I to Question God?

It may feel as if you are questioning or challenging God by reading this book. I suggest this idea is farthest from the truth. *This book and the exercises within it seek to help us become more clear about the divine and better understand the divine.* What we are questioning and examining is our understanding of the divine. The assumption we are making is that if the divine made the world and created us, any error that takes place is ours, not the divine's.

If we need clarity about human error, it is most logical to go to the source of the truth (the divine) for answers, rather than the source of the error (humans and human institutions).

This can be done without becoming hostile towards the humans and institutions that have done their best to communicate divine truth. *If we spend our energy on making others wrong, we have less energy to focus on learning from the divine.*

I, the writer, am human. It is my intention that this book comes through in the clearest way possible. If you find fault with what I (a human) write, I suggest you seek clarification from the divine rather than another human.

If you feel it is wrong to question the beliefs of your religion, perhaps you can ask the divine to help you do this process in a way that the divine supports. If you believe you need to ask for forgiveness because you feel you are questioning what you have been taught, let the divine know you only want to know how to be a better follower of divine truth. If your religious beliefs, leaders or organizations do not allow you to even question or clarify your beliefs, you may wish to consider what they have at stake that would keep them from wanting the complete truth to come out.

Let's say I am a teacher, and I tell you that you will burn your hand if you place it in the fire. You may not agree with me, so you may decide to see for yourself. If I know fire burns, I am not afraid of being wrong. If you test my belief, you will find that I'm correct. *When teachers know they are correct, someone questioning them does not threaten them. In fact, great teachers encourage questions because questions are a necessary and natural part of the learning process. Important questions ultimately lead to important truth. Additionally, the best teachers are always open to the possibility of being incorrect, so they too are open to questioning what they understand to be true. The commitment is to the truth, not the teacher.*

A true teacher is not afraid of losing his or her position of status or power. *A person who protects power, position, status, money and similar things is not a teacher, but a seeker of these things.* A person of power may be threatened if his or her so-called truths are questioned because he or she may lose his or her status if their "truths" are found to be untrue or no longer useful. There are leaders today who demonstrate this fear of losing power by their actions. Leaders who speak only about racial or ethnic tensions only have a place on stage so long as their followers believe their message. Because of this, they may be motivated to create or perpetuate racial or ethnic tensions so they keep their power and influence.

If I am a leader of people with purple-colored skin, I may say all people with blue skin are evil in order to create followers. My power will disappear the moment my followers (the purple-skinned people) make friends with the blue-skinned people. If I have nothing more to offer than prejudice, in order to survive as a leader of the purple-skinned people, I must continue to breed hate between the people so I will continue to have power.

True teachers, masters and leaders create more teachers, masters and leaders. People who seek to create followers are not leaders, but power seekers.

One other reason I may become scared if someone does not believe as I do is if I know or believe they will be hurt. Going back to the same example of the fire, I may not want to allow my child to get burned by the fire, so I may prevent them from touching the fire. But as is often seen, the child only learns *after* he or she touches the fire. The child rebels because I am preventing them from exercising their freedom. *To the child, it may seem as if I'm trying to control them – and that's because I am. The fact that I say I love them does not change the simple fact that I am trying to control them.*

I may believe my purpose is to protect them. But if my need for control becomes so excessive that I can't let the child make a move or decision for themselves, it can lead to over dependence.

So in the long run, it may be better for the child to feel the burn. I can support the child in their learning process without allowing them to get seriously hurt, and I can be there for the child with the ice to fix the burn and the hugs to help them feel better.

This is not a passive aggressive trick to get my child burned. The whole time I have told my child what I believed would happen, yet I have allowed them to exercise their freedom so they may learn to become better decision makers. Similarly, the best teachers, leaders, coaches, and friends share with us what they know, but allow us to choose for ourselves.

Of course, with issues such as sex, drugs, and violence, it may be difficult to take a softer stance. Some may say it's best to protect the child until they are "old enough to know better", while others say experience is the best teacher. I do not know the answer to questions like this, but it is my experience that there is nothing that can happen to us that the divine cannot heal and handle. For some, this answer is a meaningless and empty saying, while for others, this type of faith in the divine is all they need.

Assuming you are psychologically healthy, a friend supports you and allows you to question what they tell you without trying to control you. A great teacher, leader or coach does the same. And so does the divine.

Experiential Exercise #2

- ➢ Set an intention to connect with the divine, and invite the divine to guide you in this process.

- ➢ Close your eyes and silently breathe in and out, focusing on your breath.

- ➢ Count to 3 as you breathe in, and count to 3 as you breathe out.

- ➢ Do this for 30 seconds (5 times in and 5 times out).

- ➢ **Then declare (within you) that you wish to better know and understand the divine.**

- ➢ **Ask the divine to help you do this process in a way that the divine supports.**

- ➢ Breathe in and out for 30 more seconds.

- ➢ Notice how you feel.

- ➢ Open your eyes.

What is a Coach?

A coach is anyone who inspires you to be a better you. A coach helps you create the world you most desire, achieve your most important goals, and be the person you most wish to be.

Most people are familiar with sports coaches, and they are a good example to use. The coach for a swimmer or tennis player works with the athlete to help them perform as well as possible. A coach supports and challenges the coachee at the same time. A great coach balances supporting the coachee when outside help is needed and challenging the coachee when the coachee has the ability to help him or herself.

The best coaches accept their coachees exactly as they are, and at the same time, they invite their coachees to become an even higher version of who they most wish to be.

Great coaches can accept their coachees as they are because they see the perfection in the unfulfilled goal. They can see that the first grade child is simply a perfect, but younger, version of the future twelfth grade teenager. Great coaches enjoy the process of self-creation, and they love watching and helping others become who they most wish to be.

Great coaches love their coachees, love themselves, and they love growth. They love the processes of self-definition, self-discovery and self-mastery. They feel privileged to be part of someone else's evolutionary process. They accept, appreciate, enjoy, admire, challenge, inspire and love their coachees at every step of the process.

Simply put, **great coaches love their coachees towards growth**.

God is the best coach of all.

Experiential Exercise #3

- ➢ Set an intention to connect with the divine, and invite the divine to guide you in this process.

- ➢ Close your eyes and silently breathe in and out, focusing on your breath.

- ➢ Count to 3 as you breathe in, and count to 3 as you breathe out.

- ➢ Do this for 30 seconds (5 times in and 5 times out).

- ➢ **Declare that you wish to be inspired by your life and by this process.**

- ➢ **Ask the divine to help you do this.**

- ➢ **Be still, listen and receive any guidance that comes to you.**

- ➢ Breathe in and out for 30 more seconds.

- ➢ Notice how you feel.

- ➢ Open your eyes.

Why Not Work with the Best?

If you loved the pizza from a particular restaurant, and you wanted to learn how to make it for yourself, wouldn't you go to the master chef for advice? You could learn from the other cooks who learned from the master chef, but the master chef would be able to give you the best understanding of how to make great pizza. The other cooks might take shortcuts when they cook or they may make up their own style that doesn't create as good of a pizza. The master knows better than anyone how to select the best ingredients, what challenges to watch out for, and so on. *If you wanted a good chance of getting good pizza, you might go to one of the cooks; but if you wanted to be guaranteed of getting the best pizza, you would go to the master chef.*

The divine is the master chef who knows all about how we can create our best life. The divine knows all the possible challenges and pitfalls that await us. Many of the divine's cooks (we all are cooks of the divine on some level) offer many great suggestions about living a fulfilling life, but if we seek the most clarity possible, it is best to go to the master chef. This does not take away from the contributions of other cooks, it simply recognizes where the most accurate information comes from.

I had a very interesting experience related to this when I went to a conference on psychology. As a student of psychology, I had become very frustrated with the dogmatic ideas of certain people in the field. These people would claim their ideas were correct (based on Expert A's position) and that some other person's ideas (based on Expert B) were completely wrong. Additionally, they would say that Expert A and Expert B completely disagreed about how to treat a certain psychological disorder. Then the person who "followed" Expert A would pick one situation where it was clear for all to see that Expert A's approach worked better. This person would then declare that Expert B's entire field of research was faulty and declare Expert B incompetent or wrong – even though he or she is a person recognized by millions as a leader in their field.

When I attended the conference, I often saw the experts themselves (Expert A and Expert B) on a panel where people would place case studies before them and ask the experts how they would treat certain clients. What I heard amazed me! Expert A would sometimes say that his or her style was a more effective way of treating a particular client, and Expert B would agree. Then Expert A would say his or her style was not as effective as Expert B's style for a different client. Expert A and Expert B both respected each other's styles, and they saw the strengths and weaknesses of each. It seems their followers were not able to be so objective. (Some of these followers seem to worship these experts and believe them to be perfect, but may have never spent a single moment discussing their ideas with them).

Because the followers of these experts did not have as much information or knowledge available to them as the true experts did, the followers seemed to think they needed to defend their position and make one person right and the other wrong. Only the experts knew the greater truth.

Similarly, many religious and political leaders have argued over which ways of living are "right" and which are "wrong." These leaders often claim that they or their institution know the divine better than anyone else, so everyone should just trust them. This seems very confusing when there are so many leaders and so many traditions out there, and it can be very difficult to know which leader or group to trust. At times, "leaders" can confuse or cloud issues with their own interpretations or agendas. When there are misunderstandings, disagreements, or confusion, it is best to get clarity from the one supreme expert – the divine.

With such an approach, there would be no killing in the name of God. If we simply consult our inner wisdom, most of us would agree that it seems illogical that somebody would make something and then want others to destroy it. *It seems just as absurd that the divine would create life, and then desire that we should destroy it.* Such desires to destroy and control are human, not divine. When we are confused, and we wish to create the most powerful and positive outcome, we are best served by seeking the wisdom and guidance of the divine.

If we did, we would all be able to appreciate our different understandings of life and get a clear idea of how we might best live our life. When we need clarification, we would return to communicate with the divine – not each other. The cooks go to the master chef when there is confusion. *When we are confused and need guidance, it is most effective to go to the source of all wisdom. That source is the divine.*

Experiential Exercise #4

➤ Set an intention to connect with the divine, and invite the divine to guide you in this process.

➤ Close your eyes and silently breathe in and out.

➤ Do this for 30 seconds.

➤ **Declare that you wish to act from a place of divine wisdom.**

➤ **Ask for the wisdom to clearly see the difference between divine wisdom and human error.**

➤ Be still, listen and receive any guidance that comes to you.

➤ Breathe in and out for 30 more seconds.

➤ **Thank the divine.**

➤ Open your eyes.

How Can God Be My Coach?

Effective coaching requires that we become extremely honest about who we are and who we have been; what we like about ourselves and what we don't; and what is our source of truth and what is not. Inviting God to be our coach opens up new possibilities and new opportunities. Creating this new relationship with the divine requires new behaviors and new ways of being. If we cling to old patterns in any relationship, we are almost certain of getting the same results – positive and negative.

So what's the magical formula for having God as a coach? I don't know. I'm not aware of any magical formulas for any relationship. I treat each one of my friends somewhat differently because each one is a unique and special individual. Different people like to be treated in different ways. A good friend recognizes this, and so does a good coach.

Each of us has a unique and special relationship with the divine. There are no cookie-cutter molds for engaging in this relationship. If we are using someone else's relationship model, then we are probably not truly being ourselves in the relationship.

Many of us recognize that although we have learned much about relating from our primary role models (such as our parents or society), we may not want to repeat every part of their relationship style. We can see that there are effective and ineffective ways of relating, and we have the choice to keep what works for us and let go of the rest. *If we blindly repeat what our parents did or what society has taught us, we are certain to repeat the same failures they experienced.*

Asking the divine to coach us through life involves focusing on our unique relationship with the divine, while respecting what we've learned from others and taking the best of what they taught us. We don't have to throw out the baby with the bathwater, and we don't need to get angry with those who have taught us beliefs that no longer serve us. *We can focus on the loving intentions of those who taught us and be extremely grateful for their concern and their willingness to share with us their best understanding of divine nature. We can do this without blaming them or making them wrong, even if we have discovered an understanding of the divine that serves us better. We can understand that their intentions can be on target even if their information may be off.*

An important step to having the divine as our coach is being open to seeing where our old relationship patterns serve us and where they don't serve us. When we can see what hasn't served us, we can begin to explore our beliefs, understandings, and assumptions. If we are open-minded and openhearted in this exploration, we can learn to operate at higher levels of truth, consciousness, joy, fulfillment and bliss. Then we can let go of unproductive beliefs and patterns, and we can begin creating and living more effective ones.

Most parents would love to see their children experience more happiness, success and love than they have experienced. Most parents understand something must change in order for this to happen. In the areas of life where the parents experienced success and fulfillment, it may be very wise for the children to follow their example; however, in the areas where the parents have not experienced success and fulfillment, something different needs to be done. The child must do something his or her parent did not do and be someone his or her parents have not been. The same is true of a relationship with the divine. Relating with the divine in our old ways is certain to produce the same results we have always experienced – desired and undesired.

God becomes our coach the moment we choose to have the divine to be the one central guiding force in our life. The word "choose" is the operative word here. *If we turn to God out of fear, we have attempted to make a dictator out of God, not a coach. If we turn to God out of guilt, we have tried to make a judge of God, not a coach. If we look to God out of a desire to protect ourselves in the afterlife, we have attempted to turn the divine into an insurance policy, not a coach. If we turn to God out of a desire to fit in and be accepted by others, we have attempted to make the divine into a fashion accessory, not a coach. If we look to God because someone else tells us it's morally "right" and we wish to be better than others we have tried to make God into a soapbox for us to stand on and declare others to be wrong, not a coach.*

In each of these cases, we are not really free to choose God because outside pressure is significantly influencing us. Legally, most governments recognize that if a person is forced or manipulated into entering a contract or agreement, then the agreement is not valid. In each of the above cases, there is an element of manipulation and pressure from outside forces, so they are not truly "choices" to be in relationship with the divine. It is as if someone is psychologically holding a gun to the person's head and making them relate with the divine – under the gun holder's terms.

True choice only occurs when a person knowingly and willingly selects something. "Knowingly" means the person has all the necessary facts and information. ***The best reason for making any choice is that it is in our best interest. The choice to have the divine as the central guiding force in our life is such a choice because it is in our best interest.*** The choice is most effective when it comes from within, not when it is made because of anything that anybody else says or does. ***A genuine, one-to-one, and healthy relationship with a person is direct and involves only you and the other person, with no outside interference. A direct powerful relationship with the divine is no different.***

Inviting the divine to be our coach is simply about opening up to a unique and personal relationship with the most powerful force in the universe. It's being open to divinely inspired growth and change, being humble enough to recognize the limitations of human teachers, and being wise enough to ask for guidance directly from the source. The way in which the guidance comes may be unique for each of us. ***The divine does not need books or political or religious leaders to communicate with us. Once we open ourselves up to the divine and sincerely ask for such guidance, the divine can determine how to best communicate with each one of us.***

Experiential Exercise #5

➢ Set an intention to connect with the divine, and invite the divine to guide you in this process.

➢ Close your eyes and silently breathe in and out.

➢ Do this for 30 seconds.

➢ **Invite the divine to be the main guiding force in your life.**

➢ Be still, listen and receive any guidance that comes to you.

➢ Breathe in and out for 30 more seconds.

➢ **Make a commitment to do what you need to do and be who you need to be in order to live the wisdom you receive.**

➢ Thank the divine.

➢ Open your eyes.

One Way of Getting in Touch with the Divine

There are many ways of communicating with the divine – prayer, meditation, group services, and a variety of other methods that all can produce desired results. I have experienced these methods and others, and I find they work for me; however, there are times when I feel I need a more direct or clear answer. I sincerely wish to receive wisdom and guidance from the divine, but I find it difficult for me to achieve clarity. This inability to achieve clarity leads me to do things totally on my own when I would rather have the guidance I know I need.

A few years ago, I struggled with a decision about where I should work next. I truly wanted to do meaningful work, help others and make good money for myself. I was lost in my thoughts. My intellectual mind raced for days and weeks, and the more I tried to figure it out rationally, the worse it got. This inability to achieve clarity left me feeling extremely frustrated and somewhat hopeless. I prayed and meditated daily in the various ways I had learned from various teachers, but I still wasn't getting it.

Finally, I said a simple prayer to the divine. Actually, it didn't really feel like a prayer – at least not the type of prayer I remember learning when I grew up. (It was my understanding that prayers were supposed to be requests made to the divine). It wasn't a request, but it wasn't a command either. It was more like a declaration of my state of being. I prayed, "God, I'm extremely open to whatever is the best thing for me to do, but I'm very confused. Some teachers tell me to beg you for what I want, while others tell me to command you to give me what I wish, and others say that I am you. I don't know what the full truth is, and maybe I don't need to know right now, but what I do need is clarity. I want to do your will. I want to do the highest good, and I want to be the highest version of myself. I want to be happy, kind, joyous, fulfilled, helpful, loving, and all other similar things, and I want to experience these things in my work as well as outside of my work. I am completely open, but I am confused. *Please 'hit me over the head' with the truth. Make it so clear I can't help but know what's best for me. And if that doesn't work, please make it even clearer until I understand. I want to understand. I long to understand. I acknowledge that the reason I do not understand is not your fault, but a limitation on my part. Please communicate to me in a way that I may completely understand."*

There are two reasons I like the phrase, "Hit me over the head with the truth." First, it requests complete clarity about what would be the highest choice. I am letting go of my agenda, since it may not be what is totally best for me, and seeking simply to receive the wisdom and guidance to do what is truly best for me. I'm looking to align my agenda with the divine's. I want to do this not because it is morally "right," but because I know it is what is best for me. *I choose to seek guidance from the wisest being in the universe because it makes the most sense to me.*

When I first did this, questions I had never thought of or considered started arising from within me. These questions helped me get clear about what I most wanted to do and who I most wanted to be. I had a very strong sense that there were no right or wrong answers to the questions. They were simply helping me get clear about what I most wanted to co-create in my life with the help of the divine. It was if the divine was saying, *"You have the answers you seek. I am simply helping you get quiet so you can clearly hear your inner voice."* I felt an amazing sense of peace, clarity and calm as I made my decisions, and each decision I made led me closer to being where and whom I most wanted to be.

Every time I repeated this process it worked for me. Every time! I always left feeling centered, secure, and powerful. I had a very strong sense that the divine was supporting me. This isn't to say every idea I had was perfect, or that every insight miraculously fixed every challenge I've faced in my life, or that I could pick lottery numbers. I simply knew I had the divine's support, which helped me co-create powerful results with powerful actions.

The second reason I like the phrase, "Hit me over the head with it," is that ***getting hit over my head can lead me to temporarily lose my intellectual reason. I want this. It is my reason – my "human" intellectual mind – that makes things so confusing for me. My intellectual mind becomes attached to old thoughts and ideas and prevents me from coming to an effective and powerful resolution, so I seek higher guidance.***

My intellectual mind is like a computer that has been programmed in a certain way. It seems it can only operate at the level of its programmer – me. It has limitations that its creator –

the divine – does not. There are times when I do just fine operating within my intellectual mind, but at other times, it simply does not have the answers I seek.

The problem is that my intellectual mind usually will not admit when it does not know. It tries to convince me how smart it is and how much it knows; however, after I repeat the same unproductive pattern a few times or a few thousand times, I decide to go to the source for the answers. ***Once I know how to receive guidance from the source, I do not need to know everything. I just need to know how to get what I need and trust I will be able to get it.***

I once heard that Albert Einstein said he did not waste his energy remembering his own phone number when he knew he could find it in the phone book. ***Once you can go to the divine for what you need and trust the guidance you receive, your need to spend time and energy thinking and figuring life out gets smaller, and your life becomes easier.***

Experiential Exercise #6

- ➢ Set an intention to connect with the divine, and invite the divine to guide you in this process.

- ➢ Close your eyes and silently breathe in and out.

- ➢ Do this for 30 seconds.

- ➢ **Ask the divine to make things clear to you so you may understand exactly what is best for you and what will lead to the highest good for you and everyone else in the world.**

- ➢ **Declare that you'll use this understanding to make your life and the world a better place.**

- ➢ Be still, listen and receive any guidance that comes to you.

- ➢ Breathe in and out for 30 more seconds.

- ➢ Make a commitment to do what you need to do and be who you need to be in order to live the wisdom you receive.

- ➢ Thank the divine.

- ➢ Open your eyes.

How Does this Fit with My Religion?

Seeking guidance from the divine (or nature or however you choose to refer to the source of life and creation) fits in perfectly with most mainstream religions; however, many religions are not used to the idea of having a direct relationship with the divine or they believe a middle person (or institution) is necessary to complete the connection. It's as if the message is, "seek to connect with the divine on your own (through prayer, meditation or other practices), but don't forget about the institution or else your connection will not be as good."

In their greatest forms, religious institutions and similar organizations facilitate the connection between their individual members and the divine, increase the power of the connection, and maintain the consistency of the connection. In their worst forms, they are promoted as a substitute for the connection with the divine, a gatekeeper preventing connection with the divine unless some money or power is granted them, or a distraction from the divine.

At one time in history most people thought individuals should not have access to divinely inspired books, but rather they should get the information from a middle person. As time has progressed, many cultures have evolved to the idea that individuals have the right to access these books for themselves. The connection with the divine is no different. *Each individual has the "God-given" right to access the connection with the divine.*

There's a popular saying about connecting with the divine...*when you say you talk to God, you are commended. If you say God talks back, you are committed* (to an institution for the mentally insane).

It's not crazy to think it's possible to communicate with the divine, and it's not necessary to hear voices in order to see how a divine force is supporting you in your life. Many people believe "everything happens for a reason" or that a divine force is supporting them, yet they seem to think it is disrespectful, blasphemous or wrong to ask that same divine force for insight into how they might best live their lives. *Perhaps the reason many people have not received clarity about their relationship with the divine is because they have not asked. If we feel something is worth receiving, then it must certainly be worth asking for.*

"Ask and you shall receive."

Experiential Exercise #7

➢ Set an intention to connect with the divine, and invite the divine to guide you in this process.

➢ Close your eyes and silently breathe in and out.

➢ Do this for 30 seconds.

➢ **Declare that you wish to be inspired by the divine without making anyone else wrong.**

➢ **Ask the divine to help you see how to best express your spiritual and / or your religious beliefs in the most harmonious and loving way.**

➢ Be still, listen and receive any guidance that comes to you.

➢ Breathe in and out for 30 more seconds.

➢ Make a commitment to do what you need to do and be who you need to be in order to live the wisdom you receive.

➢ Thank the divine.

➢ Open your eyes.

Enhancing Your Life Though Your Current Belief System

Whatever your beliefs are about divine reality, a daily connection with the divine will make them even more real in your life. Many great truths taught in religious or other organizations are never put into practice by their members. Without the actions to support them, these truths are merely nice ideas.

If we would live out these ideals, there would be no starvation or hunger in the world, and people would not steal from or lie to each other. *Few   major world religions look to create starvation, stealing or lying, yet their members' actions do create these things.* Connecting with the divine helps us live out the inspiring truths that are the foundation of the belief systems we hold.

Any religious or spiritual belief system that has a loving and nurturing divine being as its source will be enhanced by connecting with that divine being more deeply and more regularly.

Experiential Exercise #8

➢ Set an intention to connect with the divine, and invite the divine to guide you in this process.

➢ Close your eyes and silently breathe in and out.

➢ Do this for 30 seconds.

➢ **Declare that you wish to enhance the effectiveness and power of your religious and / or spiritual beliefs with this book.**

➢ **Ask the divine for the courage to take the actions necessary to live out your highest religious and / or spiritual ideals.**

➢ Be still, listen and receive any guidance that comes to you.

➢ Breathe in and out for 30 more seconds.

➢ Make a commitment to do what you need to do and be who you need to be in order to live the wisdom you receive.

➢ Thank the divine.

➢ Open your eyes.

Inviting the Divine to Be Your Coach

Once you have decided you are ready to have the divine be the central guiding force in your life, there is only one thing left to do – declare your intention and share it with the divine. There are an infinite number of ways to word your intention. One of mine goes like this:

God,
Lead me as I move towards a more mature understanding of myself.
Guide me as I use your gifts to help myself and others grow in wisdom, abundance and love.
Remind me that you are always with me and in me.
Help me to be the most divine human being I can be.

There are an infinite numbers of "right" ways to invite the divine into your life. This is merely one of them. You may choose to create your own intention or you may borrow from someone else. *What is most important is that you have a clear idea what YOU mean by your intention. It is also critical that the intention is yours (not just someone else's words that mean nothing to you).*

There are millions of wonderful prayers, affirmations, chants and other declarations that are immensely powerful when used by some but appear to be ineffective when used by others. The driving forces behind these communications with the divine seem to be the person's understanding of the words used and the intention behind their words. Without the fuel of gasoline, the fastest car in the world is a lifeless piece of metal on wheels. *Without the fuel of personal passion and commitment, the most popular prayer in the world is simply a collection of words.*

If I don't know what I'm asking for, how can I expect to get it? If I go to a restaurant and can't communicate what I want I will either starve or I will just get whatever they give me. I might tell others that the service or the food at the restaurant was horrible, but the truth is I got exactly what I asked for. If I don't understand the words I'm praying, chanting or saying, I may have no idea what I'm asking for. I also have no idea what I really want, so it may pass right in front of my eyes (because I asked for it), but I may not be able to perceive and receive it because I don't understand what I asked for.

If I only use someone else's words as a magic formula, but I don't believe in them or have the intention of supporting the words by who I am and what I do, I am merely wishing. Marriage vows or other promises mean nothing if the actions by those who make them go against the promises made. If I want my communications with the divine to be the most powerful, I must commit to becoming the person and taking the actions that align with my intentions. *Words alone are meaningless. Words with commitment, passion and action can change the world.*

Experiential Exercise #9

- ➢ Set an intention to connect with the divine, and invite the divine to guide you in this process.

- ➢ Close your eyes and silently breathe in and out.

- ➢ Do this for 30 seconds.

- ➢ **In your own words, invite the divine to be your coach, your guide, your mentor, or whatever word works best for you.**

- ➢ Be still, listen and receive any guidance that comes to you.

- ➢ Breathe in and out for 30 more seconds.

- ➢ Make a commitment to do what you need to do and be who you need to be in order to live the wisdom you receive.

- ➢ Thank the divine.

- ➢ Open your eyes.

Getting Coached by the Divine

I have discovered a simple process for getting in contact with the divine part of myself, which uses some simple tools found in many spiritual and religious traditions. I did not invent this. There is no patent on it. It is not the only way. It is simply a way that works amazingly well for me. It has changed and is changing my life positively forever.

The steps in this process are *Intend Connection, Connect in Silence, Declare, Ask, Receive, Specific Action, Commit, and Gratitude*.

1) *Intend Connection* – Create an intention to connect with the divine and to align your actions, feelings, thoughts, and commitments with the divine so you might better serve others and yourself.

2) *Connect in Silence* – Be still, forget what you think you know, and quiet your mind. Breathe in and out slowly and gently. Feel the presence of the divine as you breathe.

3) *Declare* – Declare what you wish to be, do, experience, or have.

4) *Ask* – Ask the divine to support you in understanding how to achieve that.

5) *Receive* – Be still and listen to your inner wisdom (that still, small voice within) to get your answers.

6) ***Specific Action*** – Ask for a specific way that you can direct your actions, feelings, thoughts, and commitments towards the outcome you seek.

7) ***Commit*** – Decide to act upon the insight you receive and abandon all excuses. *

8) ***Gratitude*** – Thank the divine for the guidance, insight, wisdom, life and support you receive.

Any answer(s) or perceived guidance derived from the use of these methods should not be followed if it (1) harms any person or person(s), (2) violates any local, state, federal or international law. Neither the author nor the publishers shall be liable or responsible to any person or entity for any loss or damage caused, or alleged to have been caused, directly or indirectly by the information or ideas contained, suggested, or referenced in this book.

It is the author's intention that this work leads the reader to a more powerful, personal, and practical relationship with the divine. The author believes the divine is the source of the answers he receives, and suggests that readers arrive at their own conclusions after using the techniques.

The whole process takes as little as 1 or 2 minutes. If it is supported by your actions, feelings, thoughts, and commitments, you can change your life forever.

You may use the process as often or as seldom as you like. Like exercising, the benefits you receive may reflect how often you use this process and how well you implement the wisdom you receive.

Here is an example of how I am using the process right now.

1) **Intend Connection** – *"God, my intention is to connect with you and with divine truth. Please guide me in your ways and truths."*

2) **Connect in Silence** – I took 5 deep breaths in and out and said (internally) to the divine, *"Guide Me"* with each breath until I was still. At one time in the process, I felt I was getting into my head and my intellectual mind (rather than accessing my deepest wisdom) so I breathed some more until I felt comfortable again.

3) **Declare** – *"I wish to communicate eternal truth in this book to help others and myself better understand how we may best serve each other and ourselves."*

4) **Ask** – *"How can I help the readers of this book experience this powerful wisdom without tainting the message or pretending to be an authority on divinity?"*

5) **Receive** – I received the following message from my inner wisdom – *"Be honest and state that you have asked for truth to come through you, but you are not the source of the truth. Also, invite the readers to access their own inner wisdom to see how true these words are for them. Try to*

convince no one. Merely share what you know to be true for you."

6) **Specific Action** – I then asked, *"How should I do this?"* and my inner wisdom told me, *"Declare that everyone who reads this book has the power to write their own book of divine and eternal truth if they will simply go inside and sincerely seek that truth."*

7) **Commit** – I committed to doing this and wrote the above words.

8) **Gratitude** – I then thanked the divine for the guidance, wisdom, and support I received. Then I received the message, *"I always have and always will give to you when you ask. There are no formulas or requirements to how you must ask, and the process in this book is not better than any other. It will serve you to ask consciously. You ask for what you want with your actions, thoughts, emotions and commitments. With the process in this book, you are simply asking more clearly. This will serve you as long as you notice all the ways you 'ask' for and receive the things, circumstances and experiences you receive. You are always asking, and I am always giving – whether you ask consciously or not."*

Experiential Exercise #10

➤ Set an intention to connect with the divine, and invite the divine to guide you in this process.

➤ Close your eyes and silently breathe in and out.

➤ Do this for 30 seconds.

➤ **Declare that you wish to receive all of the benefits available from connecting with the divine.**

➤ **Ask the divine to help you become comfortable communicating with the divine through this process.**

➤ **Ask the divine to help you know specifically how you can make this desire come true.**

➤ Be still, listen and receive any guidance that comes to you.

➤ Breathe in and out for 30 more seconds.

➤ Make a commitment to do what you need to do and be who you need to be in order to live the wisdom you receive.

➤ Thank the divine.

➤ Open your eyes.

How Will I Know It Is God Guiding Me?

We are often disappointed when we look for guarantees to validate that we are following the most divine path. No loud sirens go off when we are the on path that is best for us. There are not a devil and an angel standing on our shoulders and waiting for us to choose between like in some cartoons, and there is no green or red traffic light telling us to move forward or to turn around and move away from our current or intended path of action. *If we look only for obvious outward signs, we may quickly feel abandoned by the divine, confused or disappointed. It can be easy for us to convince ourselves the divine doesn't know about us, doesn't help us, or simply doesn't care about us.*

There are no easy-to-see obvious signs of our spiritual progress... and yet there are. The outward signs we seek may seem to escape our attention or simply not exist; however, there are an abundance of inward signs that are as easy to see as a red stoplight, when we are open to seeing them. We simply may not be looking in the right place or we may not be aware of what we are looking for.

Try this. Place one hand in front of your face and one behind your head. On each hand, wiggle your index finger back and forth, as if to say "no." You can easily see and receive the message from the hand in front of your face, but you cannot receive the message behind your head if you only rely on sight. Now turn your head so you can see the hand behind your head. The message is now visible and understandable. The message has been there the entire time, but it only becomes real to you when you receive it. Once you can learn to "see" and receive the internal signs from the divine, you will feel much more confident about your progress.

Eventually, you will see the results of your work internally and externally. These results will support or not support the choices you are making and the guidance you are receiving. The most difficult part is that it may be extremely difficult to get validation or approval from others for your progress, for a couple reasons.

First, some people will tell you it's not possible to connect with the divine. You will need to know that you are making the progress you need to make and that your intentions are pure and clear (by your definition). *If you are truly comfortable with your motives for connecting with the divine and you are experiencing the benefits of connecting, other people's opinions will probably not bother you very much.*

Second, if you share the direction you're receiving from the divine with others, they may want to interpret your guidance for you. This may not be very helpful as it is your journey, your messages and your guidance – not theirs. *You and the divine know you best, so it may serve you to keep your focus and your messages to yourself.* If you do share with others, you may want to notice how others either support you or try to pull you down. You will eventually learn who supports you and your growth and who does not. (***Ultimately, the only being who will always support you 100% is the divine***).

As you begin to see your life turning into the positive, growing, nurturing, and loving experience you hope for, you will not need validation or approval from others. Your life and your experience of it will reflect the effectiveness or ineffectiveness of your connection with the divine. You will still never be able to prove it to anyone else, but then, you won't need to.

Experiential Exercise #11

> ➤ Set an intention to connect with the divine, and invite the divine to guide you in this process.

> ➤ Close your eyes and silently breathe in and out.

> ➤ Do this for 30 seconds.

> ➤ **Declare to the divine that you wish to live by divine wisdom and guidance.**

> ➤ **Ask the divine to help you become comfortable living your life from your inner spiritual guidance rather than the opinions of others.**

> ➤ Ask the divine to help you know specifically how you can make this desire come true.

> ➤ Be still, listen and receive any guidance that comes to you.

> ➤ Breathe in and out for 30 more seconds.

> ➤ Make a commitment to do what you need to do and be who you need to be in order to live the wisdom you receive.

> ➤ Thank the divine.

> ➤ Open your eyes.

How Do I Know I'm Connected?

There is no guaranteed way to prove a person is connected with the divine, but there are many ways of knowing for yourself. When we are connected with the divine, we feel many divine-like feelings at the same time.

Some of the divine-like feelings we may experience include:

Peace	*Calmness*	*Joy*
Compassion	*Acceptance*	*Freedom*
Centeredness	*Knowingness*	*Bliss*
Abundance	*Affluence*	*Creativity*
Wisdom	*Timelessness*	*Purpose*
Unconditional Love	*Oneness with the Universe*	

These are just some of the feelings we may experience when we connect with the divine. We may also feel certain sensations in parts of our body that let us know we are connected. Some people feel a sense of love in their heart, while others feel a tingling sensation in their head. Other might feel sensations throughout their entire body.

The more you connect with the divine, the more you will become familiar with how it feels for you when you are connected. This will allow you to become better at knowing when you are receiving guidance from your spiritual mind, as opposed to your emotional (feeling) or intellectual (thinking) minds.

Experiential Exercise #12

- ➤ Set an intention to connect with the divine, and invite the divine to guide you in this process.

- ➤ Close your eyes and silently breathe in and out.

- ➤ Do this for 30 seconds.

- ➤ **Declare to the divine that you wish to always be aware of when you are connected and when you are not.**

- ➤ **Ask the divine to help you know when you are not connected so you may take the opportunity to re-connect.**

- ➤ Ask the divine to help you know specifically how you can make this desire come true.

- ➤ Be still, listen and receive any guidance that comes to you.

- ➤ Breathe in and out for 30 more seconds.

- ➤ Make a commitment to do what you need to do and be who you need to be in order to live the wisdom you receive.

- ➤ Thank the divine.

- ➤ Open your eyes.

Are You Feeling Connected or Disconnected?

As you read the following words, really internalize them and experience them. Remember the times you have felt this way.

When we are not aware of our connection with the divine we can feel disconnected, alone, insecure, afraid, judged, uncomfortable, edgy and other similar limiting feelings. We engage in our addictions in an attempt to escape our feelings and our reality. If we could just get away for a little while, we would feel so much better. But we can't. We're trapped in our own private hell as we walk around the earth. Nothing seems to be working right for us, and everything seems to be stacked against us. It's as if the world is against us, trying to bring us down. We argue with our friends, our loved ones and our co-workers. Nobody wants to be around us and we feel so lonely. The news just confirms how horrible the world is, and we know that tomorrow isn't going to be any better. We feel anxious and worried about every little detail of life. We are afraid about what might happen tomorrow, and we beat ourselves up over what happened yesterday. We stay up at night worrying and spend the day obsessing. Life appears able to only produce misery. Life is miserable.

After reading about feeling completely disconnected from the divine, how do you feel?

Are you relaxed or short of breath?

Is your heart beating slowly or quickly?

Are you feeling calm or anxious?

Do you feel comfortable or uncomfortable?

Do you feel empowered or disempowered?

Think about your grandest goal...do you think you can do it?

Think about your greatest fear...does it concern you more or less than usual?

How close do you feel to the divine?

Now, as you read these words, really internalize them and experience them. Remember the times you have felt this way.

When we are completely aware of our connection with the divine, everything feels great. We feel relaxed, comfortable, safe, confident, loved, secure, supported, accepted, and a variety of other positive and expansive feelings. These feelings lead us to take action powerfully and confidently. We are strong when the divine is working through us, and we feel a sense of purpose and meaning that we lack otherwise. Everything seems to be working for us, and we feel like an athlete who is "in the zone." The universe is doing everything possible to help us and support us in all we do. We know we can't fail, so we succeed. Our confidence is so contagious that we positively impact all those around us. People are drawn to us and want to spend time with us. Abundance naturally beats a path to our door, and we feel at one with everything and everyone. We can let go of anything because we know the divine is always here to guide us and provide for us. We live fully in the present moment because we are not feeling sorry about the past or worrying about the future. We sleep well at night, and we wake up full of energy. Life is full of wonder. It's wonderful.

After reading about feeling fully connected with the divine, how do you feel?

Are you relaxed or short of breath?

Is your heart beating slowly or quickly?

Are you feeling calm or anxious?

Do you feel comfortable or uncomfortable?

Do you feel empowered or disempowered?

Think about your grandest goal…do you think you can do it?

Think about your greatest fear…does it concern you more or less than usual?

How close do you feel to the divine?

Feeling connected or disconnected with the divine can make all the difference in the world. It can determine whether or not we have the confidence, energy, and focus to achieve our greatest goals or repeat our biggest failures. The outcome will depend on whether or not our state of being promotes or prevents our success.

Opportunity + Our State of Being = Outcome

If we spend the majority of our time disconnected, we reduce the odds that we will be successful because our state of being will prevent it. If, however, we are connected most of the time, our opportunities will usually turn into successes.

We all have opportunities. The most successful, fulfilled, and happy people make the most of their opportunities. It may be true that some people appear to have more opportunities than others, but that means nothing if the opportunities are not used.

Staying connected with the divine maximizes our chances of taking advantage of all the wonderful opportunities that come our way. When we do this, life is full of meaning, abundance, excitement, success and fun.

Experiential Exercise #13

- ➢ Set an intention to connect with the divine, and invite the divine to guide you in this process.

- ➢ Close your eyes and silently breathe in and out.

- ➢ Do this for 30 seconds.

- ➢ **Ask the divine to help you know when you are not connected by allowing you to feel some feeling in your body or some other clear and obvious sign.**

- ➢ **Declare that you will go inside and reconnect for 5 seconds whenever you feel this feeling.**

- ➢ Ask the divine to help you know specifically how you can make this desire come true.

- ➢ Be still, listen and receive any guidance that comes to you.

- ➢ Breathe in and out for 30 more seconds.

- ➢ Make a commitment to do what you need to do and be who you need to be in order to live the wisdom you receive.

- ➢ Thank the divine.

- ➢ Open your eyes.

The Best Time and Place to Connect with the Divine

We can connect with the divine anytime we wish and anywhere we choose. ***The best time to connect with the divine is right now. The best place to connect with the divine is right here.***

The divine is everywhere. The divine does not exist in only one particular place, so we do not need to be in a specific location to connect with the divine. We can connect with the divine inside "holy buildings" and outside of them, too. We can connect with the divine in a shopping mall, at a stoplight, while we're waiting for a cheeseburger at a fast food restaurant or anywhere else.

We can even connect with the divine in places we don't usually associate with the divine. In fact, these may be some of the locations where we most need to connect with the divine. The divine is always ready and willing to connect with us wherever we are. Many members of substance recovery programs like Alcoholics Anonymous and Narcotics Anonymous have found their connection to the divine when they were living out on the streets or in less desirable places. The divine created the universe. ***There is no place on earth so horrible that the divine cannot reach us if we are open, and there is no place on earth so magical that it guarantees a connection with the divine if we are not open.***

The divine is present in every present moment. There is no time that the divine is not available for connection. Saturday and

Sunday are no better times for connecting with the divine than any other. We may choose to set aside time for our rituals on these days because we wish to gather as a community and celebrate our connection with the divine, and we may experience remarkable transformation as a result. But *we are mistaken if we believe we have to wait for a special day or time to connect with the divine.*

In fact, many of us have convinced ourselves that we only need to connect with the divine for an hour every week at a religious service. For that 1 hour, we live our life by a high code of morals and ethics that are designed to spread love, joy, acceptance, and happiness in the world. Then we live the other 167 hours of our week by a different code – a code that is almost directly opposite to the code of the 1 hour we spent in our service.

We can maximize the effectiveness of the other 167 hours of our week by finding ways to connect with the divine in our everyday lives. If we do this, any time we choose to spend in community, spiritual or religious services can be that much more powerful and meaningful. If we find we do not live by the code we profess in the 1 hour we do spend in our place of worship, we may ask the divine to help us get clear about how we might best learn to live the code we profess and the type of life we most with to live.

Experiential Exercise #14

- ➤ Set an intention to connect with the divine, and invite the divine to guide you in this process.

- ➤ Close your eyes and silently breathe in and out.

- ➤ Do this for 30 seconds.

- ➤ **Declare to the divine you intend to maintain and be aware of your connection at all times and in all places.**

- ➤ **Ask the divine to help you do this.**

- ➤ Ask the divine to help you know specifically how you can make this desire come true.

- ➤ Be still, listen and receive any guidance that comes to you.

- ➤ Breathe in and out for 30 more seconds.

- ➤ Make a commitment to do what you need to do and be who you need to be in order to live the wisdom you receive.

- ➤ Thank the divine.

- ➤ Open your eyes.

Staying Connected

If you could maintain a constant connection with the most powerful, abundant, nurturing, loving, and wise force in the universe, would you? The answer seems so obvious, yet for most of us, our actions say "no." Perhaps this difference between our intention to be connected and our actual actions relates to our ideas of what it means to be connected.

We don't have to be in any particular form of worship, prayer, meditation or any other formal practice to connect with the divine. We simply need to ask and to be aware. We could pause for 15 seconds to take a few deep breaths and think of the divine. We might close our eyes and silently express gratitude for our life and all our blessings or we might say a favorite prayer or chant that reminds us of our connection with the divine.

One way of remembering is to wear something to remind you of your connection with the divine. If you wear a special ring or piece of jewelry, you can become aware of your connection with the divine each time you see it or feel it. The item doesn't need to be expensive or flashy. It simply needs to remind you.

Another way to remind yourself is to have items present in your home or place of work that remind you of your connection. These items can be anything from a beautiful picture of the ocean to items of religious or spiritual importance that help you increase or express your connection with the divine.

Another way is to use noises as reminders. If you have a watch or clock that makes sounds on a regular basis, you might remember your connection with the divine every time it makes a noise. This could be every hour, every 15 minutes or any other amount of time. It simply depends on how often we wish to be reminded of our connection. *Every time we connect, our lives get better. If we connect all the time, only the divine knows how wonderful our lives can be.*

When we connect with the divine, we feel centered, calm, powerful, loving, kind, generous, abundant, and a million other wonderful things. As we spend more time connected, we spend more of our life in the state of being we most desire. This state of being helps us to be more creative, effective, loving, confident and successful – which leads us to feel even better about ourselves and the divine.

There is no limit to how often we can connect with the divine – other than always. We don't have to stop what we're doing. When we're working we can remember to be thankful for our job, and we can take time to think of our loved ones and send them blessings through the divine. *We can be aware of our connection with the divine and the rest of the universe in any moment and at every moment.*

Staying connected with the divine is just a way to invite the most powerful and loving force in the universe to support and guide us. The divine is available 24 hours a day, 7 days a week. The only question is, "How often are we?"

Experiential Exercise #15

- ➤ Set an intention to connect with the divine, and invite the divine to guide you in this process.

- ➤ Close your eyes and silently breathe in and out.

- ➤ Do this for 30 seconds.

- ➤ **Ask the divine to help you know the best way to remind yourself of your connection.**

- ➤ **Declare that once you know this, you will do it as often as possible.**

- ➤ Ask the divine to help you know specifically how you can make this desire come true.

- ➤ Be still, listen and receive any guidance that comes to you.

- ➤ Breathe in and out for 30 more seconds.

- ➤ Make a commitment to do what you need to do and be who you need to be in order to live the wisdom you receive.

- ➤ Thank the divine.

- ➤ Open your eyes.

Connecting without Offending Others

All of this connecting with the divine can be done in a way that does not lead other people to feel their rights are being violated. *When we're comfortable with our connection, we don't need to influence or change anyone. We are happy to be as we are. When we are truly connecting in a powerful way, our life will show this. We will be so joyful, effective and confident that it will be obvious to everyone around us. People will seek us out and ask us to share our secret of fulfillment and enjoyment.*

It is not necessary for a man to shout out on the rooftops that he is a man. People can observe it without him saying a word. In fact, if someone has to convince us of something, we may want to look carefully at what is happening and understand why they are trying so hard to persuade us. For example, if someone goes out of his or her way to tell me how great of a friend they are and is constantly trying to persuade me to believe this, my first instinct is to wonder why all of this energy is spent on trying to convince me. It might feel like my "friend" is trying to make me believe something that really is not true.

A true friend does not need to convince us of their friendship because his or her actions speak for themselves. A true follower of the divine doesn't have the need to say anything or persuade anyone of his or her desire to follow the divine. Such people know themselves, feel comfortable with their connection with the divine, and don't need others to agree or approve. Many of our greatest spiritual teachers share this quality.

Experiential Exercise #16

- ➢ Set an intention to connect with the divine, and invite the divine to guide you in this process.

- ➢ Close your eyes and silently breathe in and out.

- ➢ Do this for 30 seconds.

- ➢ **Declare to the divine that you wish to connect in the way that is best for you without making anyone else wrong.**

- ➢ **Ask the divine to remove any need to prove others are wrong or you are right.**

- ➢ Ask the divine to help you know specifically how you can make this desire come true.

- ➢ Be still, listen and receive any guidance that comes to you.

- ➢ Breathe in and out for 30 more seconds.

- ➢ Make a commitment to do what you need to do and be who you need to be in order to live the wisdom you receive.

- ➢ Thank the divine.

- ➢ Open your eyes.

Divine Coaching for Couples, Families & Groups

Just as we can invite the divine to guide us individually, we can ask for assistance as couples, families and groups. The ideas suggested below are simply suggestions. As stated before, there is no right or wrong way to connect.

There are three parties to any couple: person A, person B, and the relationship. If person A and person B each receive and act on guidance from the divine, their individual lives will be more effective, exciting, enjoyable, and fulfilling. Similarly, if both people ask for guidance as a couple, they invite the divine into their relationship (the third party). They can invite the divine to be a supporting, nurturing, and love-inspiring force in their partnership. Doing this acknowledges the sacredness of the relationship and the individuals who participate in it.

One simple way to connect with the divine as a couple, family or group is to set aside 5 minutes to spend together every day when the members hold hands, hold each other (physically), or just get together and connect with the divine. You may decide to share an intention together, and then ask the divine to guide you (as a couple, as a family or as a group) to find the best ways to love each other and support each other in reaching your goals and living your dreams (as individuals, as a couple, as a family, and as a group).

Few couples have taken the time to discuss what is most important to them as a couple. The same is true of most families and other groups. Without such a shared vision of happiness and fulfillment, the couple, family or group may lack the direction necessary to be fulfilled and to create the life of their dreams. *When the divine is placed at the center of the relationship, the vision and direction necessary for enjoyment and fulfillment come from the connection with the divine. If the divine is the guide, and the people are receiving the guidance, no other direction is necessary.*

Experiential Exercise #17

> ➢ Set an intention to connect with the divine, and invite the divine to guide you in this process.

> ➢ Close your eyes and silently breathe in and out.

> ➢ Do this for 30 seconds.

> ➢ **Declare to the divine together that you wish to have the divine guide and positively influence your relationship(s).**

> ➢ **Ask the divine to help you live a divinely inspired life as individuals and as a couple, group and family.**

> ➢ Ask the divine to help you know specifically how you can make this desire come true.

> ➢ Be still, listen and receive any guidance that comes to you.

> ➢ Breathe in and out for 30 more seconds.

> ➢ Make a commitment to do what you need to do and be who you need to be in order to live the wisdom you receive.

> ➢ Thank the divine.

> ➢ Open your eyes.

Divine Coaching at Work

We can also bring our awareness of the divine into our workplace. We can ask for guidance to help us work in a way that is in alignment with our highest and most divine self. We can choose to bring meaning and divine purpose to our work even if the work, by itself, does not seem very spiritual.

We can ask the divine to help us see how we can bring divine qualities and energies into our workplace, and we can be a person who interacts with others from a place of divine connection. We may also ask for divine guidance as to how we may proceed with business decisions, how to create the most beneficial business outcome for all parties involved in a transaction, and any other guidance that can help us bring our divine energy into our work. *There's no greater source of wisdom, on any topic, than the divine. This includes work matters, too. When we align our work with the divine, we set ourselves up for success, enjoyment and fulfillment.*

We can do all this without upsetting others. We don't have to tell anyone of our divine connection, and we don't have to make anyone else wrong for not using their connection. When others see the peace, enjoyment, fulfillment and success we experience, they will naturally come to us wanting to know how we're doing what we're doing and being who we're being – or maybe they won't. It really doesn't matter. If we're content with the quality of our connection with the divine and the way we're living our lives, other people's opinions will matter very little.

If we really use our divine connection at work, we can experience something amazing. We can live our divine purpose in our work *and* get paid for doing it. We won't have to wait until we're outside of work to make a positive difference in the world. *We don't need to join a non-profit or charitable organization to make our impact on the world, and we don't need to travel to a foreign country. When we align with the divine, we can make the world a better place right where we are. After all, where else is there?*

Experiential Exercise #18 *

> ➤ Set an intention to connect with the divine, and invite the divine to guide you in this process.
>
> ➤ Close your eyes and silently breathe in and out.
>
> ➤ Do this for 30 seconds.
>
> ➤ **Declare that you wish to be divinely inspired in the workplace.**
>
> ➤ **Ask the divine to help you use your work to move towards your goals, dreams and divine life purpose.**
>
> ➤ Ask the divine to help you know specifically how you can make this desire come true.
>
> ➤ Be still, listen and receive any guidance that comes to you.
>
> ➤ Breathe in and out for 30 more seconds.
>
> ➤ Make a commitment to do what you need to do and be who you need to be in order to live the wisdom you receive.
>
> ➤ Thank the divine.
>
> ➤ Open your eyes.

* *This exercise is a great way to stay connected with the divine while you are at work. It can be extremely helpful to do this exercise every hour or so. Not only will it give you the spiritual benefits of feeling connected with the divine. It will also help you relax physically, quiet your mind and helps settle your emotions. This exercise, as with all the others, can quickly bring a sense of*

peace and other divine qualities into your world and into your being.

Addressing Our Addictions

For most people, being fully engaged in the present moment erases the need for anything else from life. It is possible to become so involved in whatever is going on in the moment that nothing else matters. This can be true of watching a great movie, enjoying a fun recreational activity, having a great conversation or connecting with the divine.

When we are fully aware of our connection with the divine (it's always there, we just don't always notice it), we don't need anything else to be happy. We are complete, and we feel complete. In the moment that a cigarette smoker is taking a drag, she does not need anything else. In that moment, she is complete. In the moment that an athlete is dunking a basketball, he does not need anything else. For that moment, he is complete. In each of these activities, the participant is fully present – if only temporarily. During the time of this connection, the person needs nothing else. Nothing else even exists for that moment. So why do some people choose to connect with the divine, while others use a drug, and still others engage in some form of activity?

We all feel the desire to be fully present in the world, but we have learned different ways of achieving this experience. We will tend to use the method of connecting to the present moment that most consistently produces our desired results. Cigarettes, alcohol and other similar drugs produce more consistent results for their users than any other method of being in the present moment. These users do not connect to the present moment as consistently with other methods such as connecting with the divine or doing something recreational. If they did, they would turn to these other methods more often.

There may come a point when a person relies only (or primarily) on one method of connecting to the present moment to the exclusion of all others. This person will spend their time thinking about this activity, planning it, looking forward to it, spending most of their money on it, and needing more and more of it to get the desired result – connecting with the present moment. If this way of getting in touch with the present moment is taken away from the person, he or she will experience significant amounts of pain and loss. This is an addiction. It is an attempt to escape from the real world; a desire is to get away from the pain of the past and the fear of the future.

Connecting with the divine also provides the opportunity to be fully present, but it doesn't have the negative side effects of drugs or other compulsive activities. ***Connecting with the divine costs nothing, leaves us feeling energized rather than drained, and has no harmful side effects.*** It is not an addiction so long as it is used to be more present in the real world, rather than to avoid it.

Any activity, including a***ctivities related to connecting with the divine*** (such as prayer, meditation, and this process) ***can become addictions if they are engaged in to the exclusion of*** *other necessary human activities or if they are used as a means of escaping objective human reality in a way that is harmful.*

There is an old story of a student seeking wisdom about enlightenment from his teacher. The student asks, "Master. If I meditate for 4 hours every day, how long will it take for me to experience enlightenment?"

The master replies, "Ten years."

The student asks further, "And what if I meditate for 8 hours a day? Then how long will it take?"

"Twenty years," came the reply from the master, much to the surprise of the student.

"What if I meditate 16 hours per day?" the student persisted.

"It will take you forty years," the master replied calmly, "because you will be meditating so much that you will not have time to live your life and experience enlightenment."

Many people with addictions report that their cravings (or weak moments) may be very intense, but only last for a short period of time. These cravings can become moments of success or failure for these people. For example, if a person can avoid their addiction for the duration of an intense 5-minute craving, they may be able to go the rest of the day without giving in to the addiction. Often, people with addictions will have sponsors or partners who they call when they are feeling weak. Frequently, these friends successfully help the person avoid engaging in their addiction.

Since there are times when a person might not be able to contact another person for support, it becomes critical for people with addictions to have some other source of strength to turn to when times get tough. For many of them, connecting with a "higher power" is the answer.

We don't need to have a strong addiction to call on the divine for guidance or help. Also, there are many forms of addiction, so we may want to be careful before we label other people as "those addicts." *Anything that leads us away from being present in the moment and causes us harm is a form of addiction. With this definition, almost all humans have some sort of addiction. As with all challenges, the best source for help with addictions is the being that created both the person who is addicted and the substance or activity that person is addicted to.*

The more often we connect with the divine, the more comfortable we will feel, and the more easily we will be able to use the connection to help ourselves and others. *We cannot be fully and consciously connected with the divine and crave an addiction at the same time because when we are fully and consciously connected with the divine, we have everything we need. There is nothing else we seek. In any moment we choose to connect with the divine, we choose to disconnect from whatever we may be addicted to. It's that simple. The difficult part for most of us is choosing to maintain the connection.*

Experiential Exercise #19

- ➢ Set an intention to connect with the divine, and invite the divine to guide you in this process.
- ➢ Close your eyes and silently breathe in and out.
- ➢ Do this for 30 seconds.
- ➢ **Declare to the divine that you intend to eliminate whatever prevents you from maintaining your connection with the divine.**
- ➢ **Ask the divine to remove any and all obstacles that you have placed between the divine and you.**
- ➢ **If you wish, declare your commitment that you will do this exercise whenever you feel the need to engage in any form of addictive behavior.**
- ➢ Ask the divine to help you know specifically how you can make this desire come true.
- ➢ Be still, listen and receive any guidance that comes to you.
- ➢ Breathe in and out for 30 more seconds.
- ➢ Make a commitment to do what you need to do and be who you need to be in order to live the wisdom you receive.
- ➢ Thank the divine.
- ➢ Open your eyes.

Divine Coaches and Human Coaches

Establishing a more direct relationship with the divine brings more clarity and truth into our life. It increases all the benefits we receive from other sources. *Any work we do with a therapist, coach, teacher, pastor or any other person should improve as a result of connecting with the divine.*

If you receive great benefits from someone you work with, it may be best to continue that relationship even as you begin connecting more often with the divine. It may also be beneficial to share with that person how you are using your divine connection to improve the results experienced from working with that person. *

Personally, I have engaged in both personal coaching and psychotherapy as both the provider and the recipient. *My connection with the divine enhances the benefits I receive when I am being helped by human healers and guides, and it helps me do a better job in my healing and coaching work with others.*

I sometimes have a human coach because I find it helps keep me continue my growth on a regular basis. At other times I prefer to connect only with the divine as my coach. When I am truly centered, I receive guidance from almost everyone I meet for I am able to connect with the divinity in each person.

We can intend to remain focused on the power and clarity that comes through the connection with the divine and get additional assistance from others. We do not need to reach a point where we think we know it all. Seeking feedback from others whom we respect and whose opinion we hold in high regard can help us from becoming unwisely arrogant or unwilling to explore where we may be incorrect.

Ideally, any teacher, healer, guide or coach, will work him or herself out of a job with students or clients. The goal should be to help the learner reach a point where they can apply the knowledge and wisdom they learn without needing to depend on the "guru." ***In order to avoid worshipping human teachers, it appears best to focus on the divine message or wisdom and occasionally glance at the teacher.***

* If you are involved in psychotherapy, counseling or any similar therapeutic relationship, it is advised that you not terminate treatment without consulting your therapist.

Experiential Exercise #20

➢ Set an intention to connect with the divine, and invite the divine to guide you in this process.

➢ Close your eyes and silently breathe in and out.

➢ Do this for 30 seconds.

➢ **Declare that you are open to receiving assistance from any and all divinely guided sources.**

➢ **Ask the divine to send you whatever assistance you need to help move towards your goals, dreams and divine life purpose.**

➢ Ask the divine to help you know specifically how you can make this desire come true.

➢ Be still, listen and receive any guidance that comes to you.

➢ Breathe in and out for 30 more seconds.

➢ Make a commitment to do what you need to do and be who you need to be in order to live the wisdom you receive.

➢ Thank the divine.

➢ Open your eyes.

Connecting with Your Eyes Open

Eventually, you'll be able to connect very quickly and very strongly. You can also reach a point where you can connect to the divine with your eyes wide open. As you do this, your life will become a living meditation. You can live your highest spiritual values in every moment you stay connected.

The more time you spend connected, the closer you get to living from your spiritual (divine) mind – just like the greatest spiritual teachers. Each moment you spend connected; you get closer and closer to continually living a life that reflects divine qualities:

Peace	*Calmness*	*Joy*
Compassion	*Acceptance*	*Freedom*
Centeredness	*Knowingness*	*Bliss*
Abundance	*Affluence*	*Creativity*
Wisdom	*Timelessness*	*Purpose*
Unconditional Love	*Oneness with the Universe*	

This is enlightenment. This is heaven on Earth. This is what a life-transforming relationship with the divine is all about.

Experiential Exercise #21 *

➢ Set an intention to connect with the divine, and invite the divine to guide you in this process.

➢ **Keep your eyes OPEN and silently breathe in and out for 30 seconds.**

➢ Focus on your breath and count to 3 as you breathe in, and count to 3 as you breathe out.

➢ **Declare to the divine that you wish to be connected and aware of your connection every moment you are awake.**

➢ **Ask the divine to help you maintain your connection at all times.**

➢ Ask the divine to help you know specifically how you can make this desire come true.

➢ Be still, listen and receive any guidance that comes to you.

➢ Breathe in and out for 30 more seconds.

➢ Make a commitment to do what you need to do and be who you need to be in order to live the wisdom you receive.

➢ Thank the divine.

** If you do this exercise enough, you will reach a point where you can stay connected to the divine at all times simply by breathing in the way you breathe when you perform these exercises. Your awareness of your breathing will be a reminder of your constant connection with the divine. As you breathe purposefully, you will **consciously** bring the divine into your life in **every** moment.*

Asking for What You Want

Once you become comfortable connecting with the divine, you can begin asking specifically for whatever you want. The process becomes simpler as you use it more often.

All you need to do is ask...

1) ***Intend Connection*** *with the divine.*

2) ***Connect in Silence***

3) ***Declare*** *what you wish to be, do or have.*

4) ***Ask*** *the divine to support you.*

5) ***Receive*** *wisdom from the divine.*

6) *Request and Get a **Specific Action** to help you apply the divine wisdom most effectively.*

7) ***Commit*** *to act and abandon ALL excuses.*

8) *Express your **Gratitude** to the divine.*

Experiential Exercise #22

- ➢ Set an intention to connect with the divine, and invite the divine to guide you in this process.

- ➢ If you like, close your eyes.

- ➢ Silently breathe in and out for 30 seconds.

- ➢ **Declare to the divine what you wish to be, do or have.**

- ➢ **Ask the divine to help you find the most effortless, loving and effective way to achieve this.**

- ➢ Ask the divine to help you know specifically how you can make this desire come true.

- ➢ Be still, listen and receive any guidance that comes to you.

- ➢ Breathe in and out for 30 more seconds.

- ➢ Make a commitment to do what you need to do and be who you need to be in order to live the wisdom you receive.

- ➢ Thank the divine.

Spiritual Freedom

Making God our coach is really about choosing to live a life directed by divine spirit rather than human thought or intellect. We acknowledge that the divine has the greatest understanding, wisdom, and knowledge of what is best for us. We trust in the divine and the divine part of ourselves.

This can be very uncomfortable because it may feel like our intellectual mind is so stable, precise and reliable. It may seem that choosing to be led by the divine is very uncertain because we may have only associated the divine with human religions and institutions. When we see some of the horrible things we (humans) have done in the name of God, it may seem safer to simply avoid God and religion altogether. But it will serve us best to note that *it's not the divine that is unstable and unpredictable; it's the humans, our sometime faulty interpretations of what the divine wants for us and the organizations we create.*

God has created life. Only humans have chosen to destroy it. God has given love. Only humans have given hate. God has shared truth. Only humans have shared lies.

So if we find ourselves lacking trust, we should place that mistrust in the proper place – with humans. The entire ability to make the divine our coach (as individuals and as a world) depends on our ability to fully trust the divine. Once we can do that, we can put our faith where it will best serve us – in the divine.

Our most murderous leaders have told us to put our faith in and focus on them. Our greatest and most compassionate teachers (Jesus, Buddha, Lao Tzu, and many others) *have told us to put our faith in and focus on the divine.*

Jesus did not invite people to pray to Jesus. He invited people to pray to God. Buddha did not suggest that others follow Buddha. He invited others to follow the path to enlightenment. Lao Tzu did not show his readers how to place their focus on him. He showed them how to focus on the Tao.

Once we fully trust the most powerful force in the universe, and we focus completely on being guided by it, all other teachers (like the writer of this book) become unnecessary. Such teachers may be helpful, but they are not necessary. Such teachers may be intellectually brilliant, but they do not have anywhere near the same amount of power, intelligence, or insight as the source of all life. *Human intellect pales in comparison to divine spirit.*

Making the divine our coach can free us from the need for other teachers. Then, when we no longer need them, we can safely embrace teachers and truly learn from them. Then our focus can be on the divine wisdom of the message rather than the brilliance of the messenger. Then we can truly do the work of the divine because we can distinguish a divine teacher from one who is not. *Truly divine teachers will anonymously and humbly lead us closer to the divine. Those who seek to lead us closer to their own teachings and suggest we focus more on them than we focus on our direct connection with the divine are not divine teachers, but power seekers.*

Intermediaries and "middlemen" (or middle people) are only necessary when we do not know how to connect by ourselves.

Once we can connect on our own, our teachers will still have the power that serves all of us – the power to help us connect with the divine, maintain our connection and increase our connection to create more life, love, abundance and joy in the world.

At the same time, our teachers will not have the power that does not serve us – the power to get others to follow them rather than divine guidance.

Experiential Exercise #23

- ➢ Set an intention to connect with the divine, and invite the divine to guide you in this process.

- ➢ If you like, close your eyes.

- ➢ Silently breathe in and out for 30 seconds.

- ➢ **Declare to the divine that you wish to live from your spiritual (divine) mind rather than your head (intellectual mind).**

- ➢ **Ask the divine to make it easy for you to hear and understand your inner divine guidance.**

- ➢ **Ask the divine for the courage to act on your divinely guided wisdom.**

- ➢ Ask the divine to help you know specifically how you can make this desire come true.

- ➢ Be still, listen and receive any guidance that comes to you.

- ➢ Breathe in and out for 30 more seconds.

- ➢ Make a commitment to do what you need to do and be who you need to be in order to live the wisdom you receive.

- ➢ Thank the divine.

The Hard Part

If it's so simple to connect with the divine, why don't we always do it? Why don't I always do it? Our reasons may be similar to reasons why we don't always exercise, eat in healthy ways, study for class, prepare properly for work, or meditate regularly.

Sometimes we might feel too tired to do it. Maybe we would rather do something else that seems more fun. Perhaps we resent the fact that it requires a constant and regular commitment, like exercise, and we would rather have one big session and be done with it. There are many other reasons that all seem to fall under the same umbrella – we're human.

Why do we do things that work so well and then stop doing them? Maybe it's just human nature. We may never know why, but we can know one simple thing – it does not have to be difficult.

We don't have to make things complicated with justifications or rationalizations. We can simply recognize when we don't make the time to connect and commit again to connect in the very moment we become aware we have not maintained our connection.

We will probably not gain much by beating ourselves up, blaming others, or with other such tactics. None of these strategies have helped us exercise regularly or eat better, so they probably won't help us make a more regular connection with the divine.

There may be additional obstacles to regularly connecting with the divine that may not exist in other areas of our life – guilt or shame. Some of us have been taught that the divine gets angry with us when we do not do things the way the divine wants. Others have been taught it is a sin to not maintain contact with the divine and that we must ask for forgiveness before we try to contact again.

These beliefs may or may not serve us. In order to best address them, it may serve us to connect with the divine and get our own answers from the divine. *We may wish to ask the divine if there is any reason we would ever not be welcome to communicate with the divine. The answer may surprise some of us.*

Experiential Exercise #24

- ➢ Set an intention to connect with the divine, and invite the divine to guide you in this process.

- ➢ If you like, close your eyes.

- ➢ Silently breathe in and out for 30 seconds.

- ➢ **Declare that you wish to make it easy for you to regularly connect with the divine.**

- ➢ **Ask the divine to help you do this.**

- ➢ Ask the divine to help you know specifically how you can make this desire come true.

- ➢ Be still, listen and receive any guidance that comes to you.

- ➢ Breathe in and out for 30 more seconds.

- ➢ Make a commitment to do what you need to do and be who you need to be in order to live the wisdom you receive.

- ➢ Thank the divine.

A Lifetime of Happiness, One Moment at a Time

If you went on a one-month vacation and felt relaxed most of the thirty days, you would probably say you had a relaxing vacation. If you went on a one-week trip and had fun for most of the seven days, you would probably call it a fun trip. And if you saw a 2-hour movie, and you were entertained for most of the 2 hours, you would probably say it was an entertaining movie.

If you go through life, and you are happy for most of the moments during your life, you will probably end up saying that you have had a happy life. The decision to have a happy, joyous, fulfilling and fun life is happening in every moment. *If you can remain content, only for this present moment, you will be happy always. You cannot always choose what will happen around or to you, but you can choose your response.*

Often it can be very difficult to find something to be happy about because our view of the world and our limited understanding can prevent us from seeing the miracles and the wonders of life going on right in front of us. When we are unable to see the good in the world, it really helps to have God as our coach.

We can simply connect with the divine and ask for help to see the beauty, the magic or whatever else about the situation we are in that can bring us joy. This does not mean we never wish to be sad. When something occurs that we believe is a tragedy, like the death of a loved one, we can feel our sorrow. We can feel our loss and experience the emotions that may go with it, but if we are able to connect with the divine, we can also be open to the miraculous parts of the event.

We can ask the divine to help us understand the situation more accurately or maybe even just be able to deal with it more gracefully or lovingly. We might not even feel sad if we are able to see the gift or the miracle in the event that appears to be a tragedy. *When we can clearly see the work of the divine in events that normally appear to be disasters, the events don't seem as disastrous because we know the divine is present.*

If we commit to connecting with the divine whenever we feel less than good, we open ourselves to be instantly guided and healed by the greatest force in the universe. No other person, place or thing has that same power. All the insecurities, doubts and feelings of low self-worth can disappear in a moment through the power of a connection with the divine. If you don't believe this is so, then who or what other force do you think can heal them?

The concept is simple. *Connecting with the divine allows us to feel complete in the moment. We can feel whole and know that we are enough exactly as we are right now. When we feel this, we feel peace, happiness, and joy. If we stay connected all the time, we will have a lifetime of happiness, one moment at a time.*

Experiential Exercise #25

- ➤ Set an intention to connect with the divine, and invite the divine to guide you in this process.

- ➤ If you like, close your eyes.

- ➤ Silently breathe in and out for 30 seconds.

- ➤ **For each of the 30 seconds, simply be aware of your connection with the divine.**

- ➤ **Notice how you feel.**

- ➤ **Imagine how your life would be if you felt this way all the time.**

- ➤ **Breathe in and out for 30 more seconds.**

- ➤ **For each of the 30 seconds, simply be aware of your connection with the divine.**

- ➤ **Notice how you feel.**

- ➤ Thank the divine.

World Peace

If we were all constantly connected to the divine, there would be only peace, love and harmony.

We can only control our behavior, but we can change the world with our example and our being – one person at a time.

If each of us only creates love, joy, and harmony in the world, then that is all there will be. The same is true for their opposites and everything in between. The only question is, "What type of world do you want to create?"

Experiential Exercise #26

➢ Set an intention to connect with the divine, and invite the divine to guide you in this process.

➢ If you like, close your eyes.

➢ Silently breathe in and out for 30 seconds.

➢ **Declare your intention to transform the world with your example and your being**

➢ **Ask the divine to help you see how you can contribute to peace in your home, your workplace, your community and the world.**

➢ **Ask the divine to give you the courage to take the necessary step(s) to create peace.**

➢ Ask the divine to help you know specifically how you can make this desire come true.

➢ Be still, listen and receive any guidance that comes to you.

➢ Breathe in and out for 30 more seconds.

➢ Make a commitment to do what you need to do and be who you need to be in order to live the wisdom you receive.

➢ Thank the divine.

Last Thoughts

There is no more powerful, loving and nurturing source in the universe than the divine (or whatever name you prefer).

The more often we connect with the divine, the more powerful, loving and nurturing we become.

Some spiritual teachers have spent their entire lives bathing in the ecstasy of connecting with the divine. They have and experience a peace and a love that goes beyond ordinary human understanding.

Like our greatest spiritual teachers, we all have moments when we are divinely inspired, feel connected to the entire world, and do amazing things. Our greatest spiritual teachers simply experience this much more often. Some experience it all the time.

There is no necessary external reason to connect with the divine. Doing it for fame, fortune, recognition, acceptance or any other external motive seems almost ridiculous because when we connect to the divine we do not need the approval of others or anything else outside of us.

Internal desires appear to be the best reason to connect with the divine – as often as possible. What more reason could we have than wanting to experience the fullest levels of love, kindness, compassion, peace, confidence, connectedness, bliss, and every other expansive feeling humans have ever sought to know and live.

We literally have a choice, in every moment, to live consciously connected with the divine or to be unaware of the most powerful force in the universe.

Any ceremony, person, institution, book, habit or other thing that leads us to stay connected to the divine is a true gift to us. No matter what we call it, if it leads us to divine inspiration and divine connection, surely it is divine.

Any ceremony, person, institution, book, habit or other thing that leads us to disconnect from the divine is a true obstacle or curse for us. No matter what we call it, if it leads away from divine inspiration and divine connection, it would appear to be a human error.

Experiential Exercise #27

- ➢ Set an intention to connect with the divine, and invite the divine to guide you in this process.

- ➢ If you like, close your eyes.

- ➢ Silently breathe in and out for 30 seconds.

- ➢ **Declare to the divine that you wish to fully receive the benefits from reading this book and all other spiritual books you have ever read.**

- ➢ **Ask the divine to help you find the most comfortable and effective way for you to connect regularly.**

- ➢ Be still, listen and receive any guidance that comes to you.

- ➢ Breathe in and out for 30 more seconds.

- ➢ Make a commitment to do what you need to do and be who you need to be in order to live the wisdom you receive.

- ➢ Thank the divine.

Making God Your Permanent Coach

The book is now over, but the journey is only now beginning. I honor you for your commitment to yourself and to your relationship with the divine. The simple fact that you have read this far is a powerful indicator of your commitment to this work and to your relationship with the divine.

I invite you to seriously consider what you need to do next to continue growing and experiencing the miraculous benefits of this work. Connecting with the divine is an ongoing process. A relationship with the divine is much like a relationship with anyone else. The more we invest in the relationship, the more we will benefit.

My relationship with the divine is by far the most rewarding relationship I have ever engaged in. People are great, but the divine's ability to give to us, love us, support us, and nurture us is far beyond the capacity of any human. I can honestly say every moment of my relationship with the divine has been productive, loving, nurturing, loving, supporting, and everything else I could ever ask for in a relationship. ***God has never let me down.***

The more I connect, the better my life gets. I invite you to examine what it would take to make the divine a permanent and powerful part of your everyday life. ***What would it take for you to fully allow the divine to bless, guide, and nurture your life?*** Maybe it would take connecting every hour or perhaps it would take reading a chapter of this or some other book every day.

Whatever approach you take, I invite you to check on yourself regularly and see how you are doing.

This may not be the first book you have read about the divine, but it can be the first book you read and decided to put into permanent action. I cannot stress this enough. This book, like many others, offers valuable insights and exercises for improving your spiritual life; however, the exercises are only valuable if they are done.

My intention is that you will take powerful action as you decide to make the divine a permanent part of your everyday life.

I invite you to share this work with anyone you feel is truly interested in growing in his or her relationship with the divine. At the same time, I also invite you to accept people as they are and not use this work as a way of making others wrong just because they choose to handle their relationship with the divine differently than you.

My intention is that this work becomes a tool used by billions of people to positively transform the world from the inside (the individuals) to the outside (the world). I remain open to any thoughts, ideas, or suggestions you may have that will further this process. Create a great life.

Peace,

Wade

Experiential Exercise #28

- ➢ Set an intention to connect with the divine, and invite the divine to guide you in this process.

- ➢ If you like, close your eyes.

- ➢ Silently breathe in and out for 30 seconds.

- ➢ **Declare to the divine that you wish to know how to make your relationship permanent, powerful, and life transforming.**

- ➢ Ask the divine to help you know specifically how you can make this desire come true.

- ➢ **Ask the divine to help you see what your life could be like if you acted on the guidance you receive.**

- ➢ Ask the divine to help you know specifically how you can make this desire come true.

- ➢ Be still, listen and receive any guidance that comes to you.

- ➢ Breathe in and out for 30 more seconds.

- ➢ Make a commitment to do what you need to do and be who you need to be in order to live the wisdom you receive.

- ➢ Thank the divine.

Quoting This Book

Books that address spiritual and religious issues are often quoted in other new works. Some of these new works look to build on what the previous book addressed, while many seek to tear down or prove wrong the ideas in one text in order to build up or make right other ideas or beliefs about the divine.

The fact that there are so many religious and spiritual belief systems, groups, and rituals, seem to indicate that we each experience the divine a little differently. There does not have to be only one right way to express our beliefs and ideas, and making others wrong is sure to lead to further arguing, fighting, and death – all "in the name of God."

If you are looking to quote this book, I invite you to search your heart and connect with the divine to find the answer to one simple question, "Are you looking to build upon love and invite more of God's children into a loving, nurturing, and supportive divine relationship (no matter what the details of the relationship look like) or are you looking to tear down someone else's ideas or beliefs in order to promote your own by proving someone or something wrong?" Put another way, "are you being driven by love to create more love or are you being driven by something other than love to create something other than love?"

Religious leaders and institutions are not the only initiators of division and discord. Individuals and the members of institutions also create these.

It is possible that the divine, with divine wisdom and love, accepts and loves all our attempts to love and connect with the divine, just as a mother accepts and loves the different ways each of her children attempt to love and connect with her.

If we can come to understand that the divine loves and accepts us all as we are and where we are on our path of growth, perhaps we can let go of our childlike sibling rivalries and competitions for attention. Then we can spend all our energy on connecting with the divine and loving each other.

Experiential Exercise #29

➤ Set an intention to connect with the divine, and invite the divine to guide you in this process.

➤ If you like, close your eyes.

➤ Silently breathe in and out for 30 seconds.

➤ **Declare to the divine that you wish to use this book to build divine community with others, regardless of their spiritual belief system.**

➤ Ask the divine to help you know specifically how you can make this desire come true.

➤ **Ask the divine to help you see what the world could be like if we all acted on the guidance we receive.**

➤ Be still, listen and receive any guidance that comes to you.

➤ Breathe in and out for 30 more seconds.

➤ Make a commitment to do what you need to do and be who you need to be in order to live the wisdom you receive.

➤ Thank the divine.

Acknowledgments

Thank you to every being who has ever led me closer to the divine. God, Jesus, Buddha, Lao Tzu, St. Francis, Mother Teresa, Martin Luther King, Gandhi, Rossana, Francisco, Luna, Mom, Dad, Natalie, Christian, Brad, Andrea, Madison, Mason, Matthew, Boston, Coco, Pablo, Pilar, Mariana, Gonzalo, Marianita, Gonzalito, Samantha, Santiago, Jen, Father Joe, Father Jerry, Father Jack, Father Mike, Father Guy, Ms. Campbell, the Catholic Church, St. Thomas Aquinas High School, Religious Science, the New Age and New Thought Movement, Neale Donald Walsch, Marianne Williamson, Debbie Ford, the Integrative Coaching Program Coaches and Participants, Deepak Chopra, David Simon, Wayne Dyer, Shakti Gawain, Don Miguel Ruiz, Carlos Castaneda, Marsha Sinetar, Elaine St. James, Stuart Wilde, Sean, Beckey, Christie, Stephanie, Danielle V., Tino, David Warren, Reverend Ernie Chu, John Lennon, George Harrison, Sting, all my coaching and business clients, my volleyball buddies, my friends, and everyone else I haven't mentioned.

Special thanks to Rossana, Mom, Natalie, Adam Heller, and all who helped me find the best words I could to communicate such powerful and important work.

Thank you especially to all my other "teachers." (Those people whom I have seen as devils, but whom are truly angels in disguise, teaching me about humanity and my divinity).

About the Author

Wade has led retreats and personal growth workshops, authored books on spirituality, personal growth, finance, parenting, business growth & more.

He has worked successfully as a life coach, 4-day work week mentor, organizational consultant, computer trainer, sales consultant, executive coach, speaker, mental health counselor, management consultant, software designer and programmer, author, business analyst, financial counselor, and in many other capacities.

Wade has a Bachelor's degree in Marketing and a Master's degree in Mental Health Counseling Psychology.

He lives happily with his wife and children.

His email address is wade@wadegalt.com .

Author Blog & Website

You may visit Wade's blog & website at www.wadegalt.com.

I Forgot

I forgot that I am a child of God, and I felt so afraid.

The winds outside blew hard, and I wondered if I would see morning.

Every fear that I've ever had came rushing towards me in waves.

As the waves on the beach seemed to grow bigger and nearer,

I forgot that I am loved by our creator, and I became terrified.

How could I protect myself from the dangers outside?

How would I survive without someone to take care of me?

I forgot that I'm buddies with the Almighty, and every noise kept me from my peaceful rest.

Unable to bear my vulnerability, I prayed to fall back into unconscious sleep.

Then I wrote down this poem and all of last night's dramas were forgotten.

Then when I forgot that I forgot, all was well again.

Get the Workbook & Journal for Free

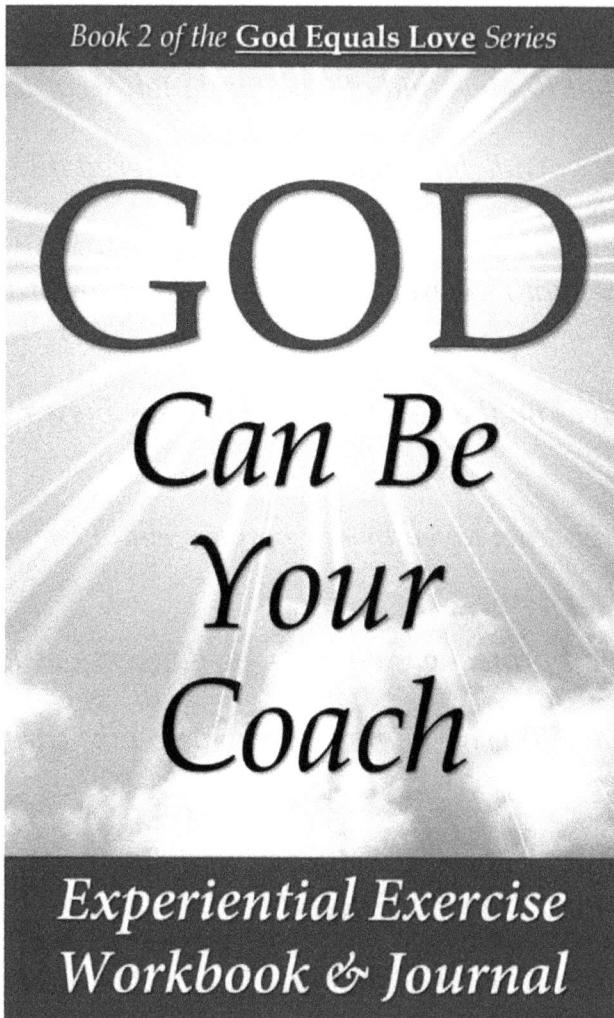

Book 2 of the **God Equals Love** Series

GOD
Can Be
Your
Coach

Experiential Exercise
Workbook & Journal

Get the exercises from this book in printable (PDF) format
so you can type or write them out and track your progress.

Go to www.wadegalt.com/gcbyc-journal

Also by Wade Galt

Put Your Money Where Your Soul Is

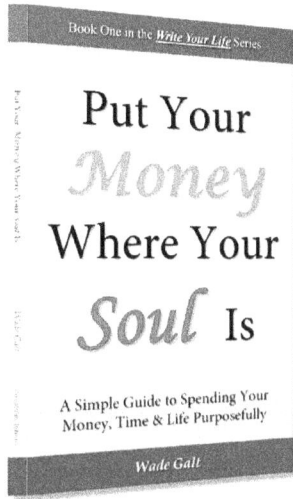

Book One in the *Write Your Life* Series

Put Your
Money
Where Your
Soul Is

A Simple Guide to Spending Your
Money, Time & Life Purposefully

Wade Galt

Mommy and Daddy Love You Exactly As You Are

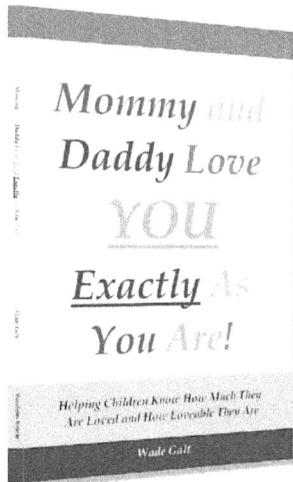

Mommy and
Daddy Love
YOU
Exactly As
You Are!

Helping Children Know How Much They
Are Loved and How Loveable They Are

Wade Galt

The *God Equals Love* Book Series

Book 1 - Divine Self-Esteem

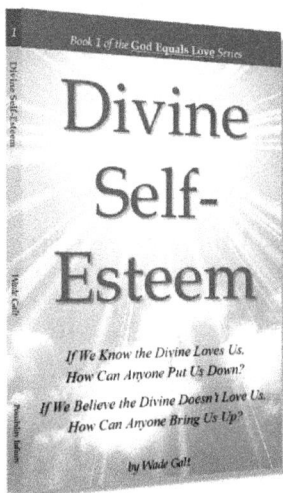

Book 3 - GOD Loves You Exactly As You Are!

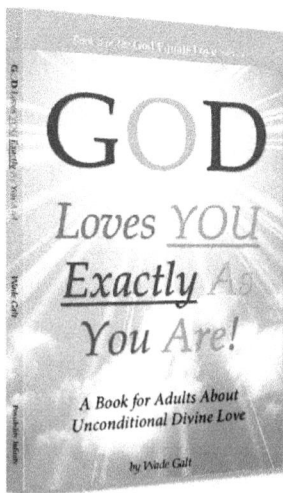

Book 4 - GOD Can Be Your Coach at Work

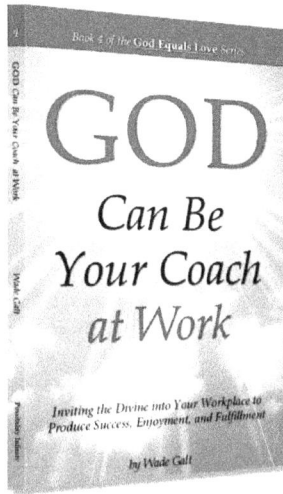

Book 5 - The Gospel of Inclusion

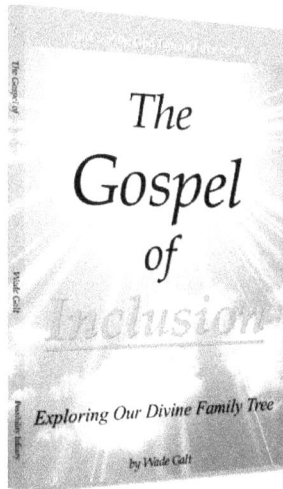

Book 6 - God Is In There

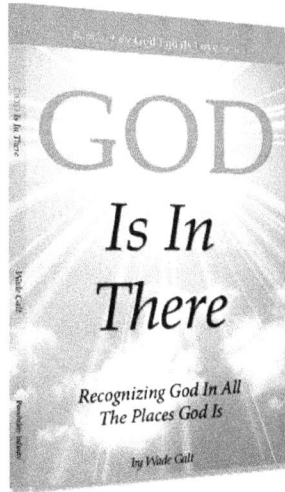

Book 7 - The Boy Who Wanted to Know God

Book 7 - The Girl Who Wanted to Know God

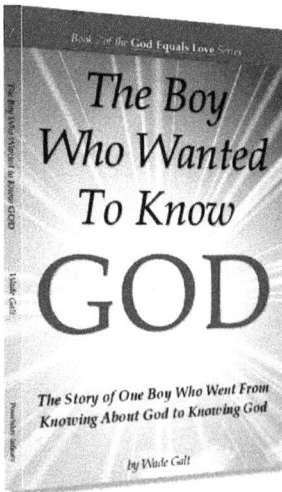
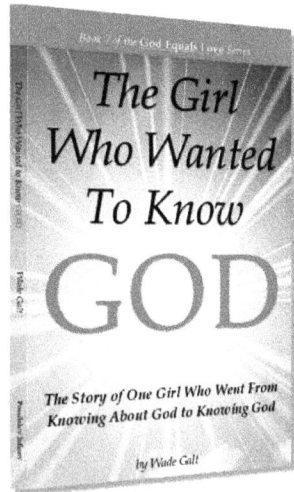

Other Books & Translated Books

Many of these books have been translated into Spanish, and there are other books also available.

To see these books and other books not listed here, visit www.wadegalt.com/books .

All profits from the sale of the GOD EQUALS LOVE books go to organizations and charities that seek to end unnecessary hunger and poverty.

New Book & Program Notifications

If you'd like to be emailed when we release new books, audios and other programs please visit www.wadegalt.com/notifiy to sign up for these notifications.

Share the Message & the Love

I hope this helps you see & feel how truly amazing and miraculous of a creation you are and how much the divine values you.

If you found the book to be helpful, would you please be so kind as to write a review on Amazon for the book or share the book on Facebook, Instagram, Twitter or other social media so others may know how it helped you?

Even if it's a super-short review, every little bit helps.

Thank you so much.

If there's anything I can do to help you further with this work, please email me at is wade@wadegalt.com .

All my best,

Wade

www.ingramcontent.com/pod-product-compliance
Lightning Source LLC
Chambersburg PA
CBHW061148040426
42445CB00013B/1605